ONE MAN'S FURR

This book is dedicated
to

My longsuffering wife, and the two in my family,
They patiently bore with me - even quite happily,
What with the fruit, and the corn, and the cattle,
And many hours spent in the Spiritual battle,
I fear that I could not have treated them decently,
One of them laughingly said to me recently,
"All I remember when I was eleven,
Is Dad rushing in from his work about seven,
A wash, and a change, and a cup of tea fast -
Then up in the pulpit before 'twas half-past!"

The Runaway, page 14

ONE MAN'S FURROW

Poems By
David Obbard.
A
Sussex Farmer
and Pastor.

The family home at Cherry Gardens.

Section Contents.

Down to Earth.
Craftsmen of the Bible.
The Life of David
In the King's Uniform
Scripture and Devotional.

All rights reserved.
Copyright © 1993 David Obbard.
Cherry Gardens Publications,
Groombridge, Tunbridge Wells,
Kent. TN3 9NY

ISBN 0 9517416 2 4

Pen and ink drawings by Sue Obbard.

By the same author; 'Countryman's Heritage'
Spiritual lessons drawn from country scenes
and the author's own experiences.
'Ploughboy to Pastor'
Early years, on the farm, and in the ministry.

CONTENTS

Down to Earth	page 7
The New Day	8
Sunsets	9
Hearts-ease	10
The Horse Plough	12
Teamwork	13
The Runaway Horse	14
A Storm at Sea	16
The Charcoal Burner	17
Summer Storm	18
The Work of Faith	19
Visit to Wales	20
The Swallow's Message	21
The Silent Presence	22
Being Retired	23
The Chapel Mouse	24
The Oil Can	26
The Country Preacher	27
Lights That Shine	28
Craftsmen of the Bible	33
Farmers and Gardeners	34
The Ploughman	35
The Sower	36
Shepherds	37
Builders and brickmakers	38
Stonemasons	39
The Carpenter of Nazareth	40
Shipbuilders and Cargoes	41
The Teacher	42
Fishermen	43
The Master-Fisherman	44
In The King's Uniform	45
The Home Guard	45
The Little Corporal	46
Attention!	47
For Such A Time As This	48
Tribute to King George V1	50

CONTENTS

The Bugle	53
The Life of David	57
Who David Was	58
The Lion and The Bear	59
David the Deliverer	60
David's Anointing	63
David Flees From Saul	64
David Becomes King	65
David's Kindness	66
David Restored	67
What David Sang (Psalm 23)	68
Scripture and Devotional	69
Christmas-time	69
The Magnificat	70
Hannah's Son	71
John 1	72
The Stranger At The Door	73
The Giving of The Law	74
The Ten Commandments	75
The Eleventh Commandment	76
The Pearl of Great Price	78
Ephesians 3 v14-21	79
Isaiah 26 v1-7	80
Isaiah 28 v24	81
Increase Our Faith	82
Gethsemane	83
Precious Promises	84
The Thorn	85
Honourable Scars	86
Sorrow And Joy	87
The Old Paths	88
Brotherly Love	89
Charity	90
Trust in The Living God	91
The Lord Looks at the Heart	92
Who Is This?	93
Loading the Vessel and Setting the Sail	94
The Song of Moses	95

DOWN TO EARTH

THE NEW DAY

The rosy glow of dawn,
The bright green grass,
The golden corn,
The singing of a bird,
A crowing cock is heard,
Another day is born.

The milking cows come in,
The dogs all bark,
An awful din;
The rising sun breaks clear,
The cloud banks disappear,
And daylight hours begin.

The foxes slink away,
The ducks all quack,
The kittens play,
The horses lift their heads,
The piglets leave their beds,
To welcome in the day.

The honey bees all hum,
Tap, Tap, I hear
Woodpecker's drum;
The skylarks take to wing,
All nature starts to sing,
"Another day has come".

SUNSETS

The sunset glory fills the sky
  With wonder, and with awe,
For there are colours in the sky
  Which no paint-maker saw.

They shimmer, glow, and pulse with life,
  In all their varied shades,
Each vies with each, harmonious strife,
  As each appears, then fades.

Whence came those palaces on high,
  Those noble towers of light?
Glorious formations in the sky
  Which fascinate the sight.

Not in a moment are they made,
  Though but a moment stay;
The mist contributes to each shade,
  With dust from far away.

And it's the sun, that mighty ball
  Of fire and energy,
Gives shape and beauty to it all,
  And makes the scene we see.

And so God gathers mist and dust,
  With wind, and storm, and strife,
Then makes, by shining as He must,
  The sunsets of our life.

HEARTS-EASE

A story is told of a mythical king
   Who went into his garden one day,
And found that the birds had forgotten to sing,
   While the plants were all dying away.
The blackbird was silent, for he could not sing
   Like the nightingales, when it was dark;
The songthrush was moping, with head under wing,
   After failing to trill like the lark.

The sturdy great oak looked as if it would die,
   Wishing it could be slim like the pine;
The pine felt cast down when it could not supply
   A source of sweet grapes like the vine.
The vine was disheartened for failing to reach
   To the sky like its neighbour, the pine,
And having no fruit as is found on the peach,
   So left off producing it's wine

And every sweet flower was hanging its head,
   Its colour and fragrance forsook,
Each wanted to be like its neighbour instead,
   And all had that withering look.
Then one little spot in the garden was found
   Which managed the monarch to please,
For there, at his feet, keeping low to the ground,
   Was the little plant known as Hearts-ease.

"Tell me", said the king, "why you're looking so bright,
   When all those around you are sad?
You don't seem the least bit distressed by the sight,
   In fact, you seem actually glad".
The Hearts-ease replied, "Though I'm nothing to see,
   You wanted me here in your plan;
And so I am thinking it's all up to me
   To be the best hearts-ease I can."

And so in God's garden, wherever you be,
   Don't fret if you're humble and small,
Don't envy the strength of the mighty oak tree,
   Or try, like the pine to be tall.
Don't ape at the vine, or the peach, or the flower,
   That somehow you rather would be,
But say to yourself throughout each passing hour,
   The Lord wanted me to be ME.

Keep praying and praising, and looking above,
   Your Maker and Master to please,
Just lift up your face to the sun of his love,
   And you will discover   Heart's ease.

The HORSE PLOUGH

Lying in a Farm museum,
See the plough, once used by horse,
Some may hold it in derision,
Think it useless, if not worse.

Those who know the simple pleasure
Of horse-ploughing on the land,
Still regard it as a treasure,
Something noble, though not grand.

As it stands upon the headland
It appears a humble thing;
Set it working in the furrow -
This transforms it to a king!

Acres of last season's stubble,
Weeds which long had rampant grown,
Earth, which through the drought of summer,
Had become as hard as stone;

Roots, which had defied all efforts,
Sending shoots up, day by day,
All must now vacate possession,
Yielding to the monarch's sway.

Where was only wild confusion
Ordered beauty now appears,
God and man unite, preparing
Harvests for the future years.

TEAM WORK

"Gidde-up Old Man", the carter said,
And the old horse bowed his noble head,
His muscles swelled as he took the strain,
And started off with a load of grain.
For there was a bond between these two
To show to the world what they could do.

"Steady now, Old Man", the carter said,
The horse leaned back on the breech instead;
He'd pulled the load with a right good will,
And now he must hold it back down-hill,
For all must learn, as they drink life's cup,
That going down can be worse than up.

"Well done, Old Man" then the carter cried,
He patted the horse's neck with pride;
The old horse loved to be spoken to,
He arched his neck, as a horse can do,
And, just to show he could understand,
He pushed his nose in the carter's hand.

"Who-a now, Old Man, and stand you still,
While we unload at the water-mill":
And the old horse stood as still as stone,
Though a dog might bark, or horn be blown,
He would not move till he once more heard
The carter give him the starting word.

The carter moved to the horse's head,
"We are going home, Old Man", he said,
And the old horse chuckled his delight
He thought of his stable, warm and bright,
With a bowl of oats, and sweet best hay,
Waiting for him at the close of day.

The RUNAWAY HORSE

We had a fine horse, an upstanding young grey,
Who'd stood in the stable for many a day;
'Twas dead of the winter, the land was ice-bound,
A deep crispy layer of snow on the ground.

My father said, "David, it's time that we found
A job for that youngster - he's fresh, I'll be
  bound":
I said,"O.K. father, we'll make him a sleigh,
And then we can bring all the cord-wood away".

For up by the road, about half of a mile,
We'd cut down some oak trees, and made a great
  pile
Of cord-wood for firing; cold weather was here
With coal on the ration, beside being dear.

We soon made the sleigh, I'll admit it was rough,
But still, it was made of substantial stuff;
We brought out the horse - what a picture he
  made!-
The strength and the beauty of nature displayed.

He looked at the sleigh as he came walking by;
A glint of sly humour crept into his eye.
We hitched up the traces; he stood like a child;
We felt much relieved, but the horse merely smiled.

"Its time to get going and fetch the first lot,"
I said: at a word he was off like a shot!
"Whoa! Steady!" I said, "for there's no need to run."
But soon it was plain he was out for some fun.

For when I decided to make the next try,
He stood on two legs, with his head in the sky.
Then down went his head, and away went his heels,
He pranced up and down despite all my appeals.

I said to my work-mate, "Here, you take his head,
I'll jump on his back and will ride him instead,
And then he can gallop away at his will.
'Twill let off some steam as he runs up the hill."

I gripped with my knees, and I gathered the rein,
With one hand I got a good grip on his mane,
Then said to the laddie, "Right! let the horse go,
We're set for a gallop way over the snow."

He stood on one side and the horse gave a jump
That nigh sent me flying back over his rump;
Then up with his back-end and down with his head
To shoot me down over his withers instead.

Like a shot from a gun, or a shaft from a bow,
That little grey horse whistled over the snow;
With head in the air, and his tail straight behind,
He scarce touched the ground as he went like the wind.

The folk by the wayside stood holding their breath
To see one so foolishly courting with death;
They did not know whether to come or to go
As I thundered by in a whirlwind of snow.

At last, to my own and the others' surprise,
I brought the horse home, and was still in one piece,
But though I had conquered, I'd no room to talk -
For the rest of the week I could scarce bear to walk!

STORM AT SEA

A ship was sailing on the sea
In sixteen ninety-nine;
It looked as grand as it could be
And everything was fine.

But soon clouds gathered in the skies,
The wind at storm-force blew,
It made the seas like mountains rise,
And terrified the crew.

It shook the ship with blast on blast,
And made the vessel toil,
It tore the rigging from the mast;
The waters seemed to boil

It blew so hard they could not steer
The ship away from shore,
And every heart was full of fear
To hear the breakers roar.

The captain called the men on deck,
He was both good and brave,
He said, "We soon must be a wreck,
Except that God can save".

"Let every man now kneel and pray,
That God will mercy show".
The wind soon turned the other way,
Into an 'off-shore blow'.

So they were saved by God, who said
"In trouble, call on me,
And though your hearts are full of dread,
I will deliver thee".

THE CHARCOAL BURNER

'Twas wintertime, with ice and snow,
Which makes a very pretty show,
But on a mountain, with his wife,
A poor man nearly lost his life.

A charcoal burner he by trade,
Who very little money made,
And so, because he was so poor,
Had very little food in store.

Another man, ten miles away,
Who lived in plenty every day,
Was, on this very bitter night,
In bed asleep, all snug and tight

But suddenly he woke in fright
And said, "Who called to me this night?
No sooner I to sleep had gone
Than someone said, 'Take food to John'".

Three times he slept; three times he woke;
Three times these very words he spoke;
Then farmer Brown said,"Wife, awake!
For I some food to John must take.

But who is John?" "Why now," said she,
"That must the charcoal burner be".
They quickly packed with food a sleigh,
And to the mountain made their way.

The journey took five hours or more,
And, when at last they reached the door,
They heard the poor man's earnest prayers
To Him who for his people cares.

That day the food had quite run out,
But faith had triumphed over doubt,
For as in prayer to God he cried
Those pressing needs were all supplied.

THE SUMMER STORM

The clouds gather darkly, the sun hides her light,
The lightning is flashing, how awesome the sight,
Great volleys of thunder roll all round the skies,
The beasts run for shelter in fearful surprise.

The wind blows a tempest, the rain falls like rods,
Straight down from the heavens, the windows of gods,
The storm grows in fierceness, its fury awoke,
And topples the elm tree, the beech and the oak.

The birds all fall silent, each muted with fear,
And all men are troubled by what they can hear;
The roar of the tempest, the lash of the rain,
Which spread such destruction o'er mountain and plain.

But then it is over, the sun shines again,
The south wind blows softly, with warmth in its train,
The rainbow shines brightly against the dark cloud,
And speaks (though it's silent) God's promise aloud.

Then all through the summer the brooks run more sweet,
The grass grows more lush for the cattle to eat,
The birds sing their music most sweetly again,
And man can rejoice in abundance of grain.

The storm has passed over, the blessing remains,
For there is a saying, "In loss there are gains,"
And folks in the country have long understood,
"It must be an ill wind that blows us no good."

For those who trust Jesus, come wind, storm, or hail,
We know that God's promises never can fail;
Though all that we view looks as bad as it could,
The Father has promised it all works for good.

THE WORK OF FAITH

"We want to Market Garden,
  but we don't know how," they said,
"We've lots of willing helpers,
  but we lack an able head."
I ploughed them up an acre,
  which was what they said they'd need,
And got the ground all ready
  for the sowing of the seed.
But then they said, "An acre
  is much more than we can do;
We'll have about a quarter,
  and then leave the rest to you."

The ground was quickly planted,
  or the various seeds were sown,
And much enthusiasm in this
  pleasant work was shown.
Then I went down with hoe in hand
  to see the work one day,
And found the willing helpers
  were all sitting down to pray;
They said, "Come here and join us
  as we ask the Lord to bless,
For prayer is most important
  if we're looking for sucess."

I said, "That is important,
  for I do believe in prayer,
But weeds will keep on growing
  if I come and join you there."
They prayed to God sincerely
  for His blessing on the seed,
But never did I see a hoe
  at work among the weeds!
I prayed as I was hoeing,
  and a healthy crop was grown:
They prayed without the hoeing –
  and reaped nought from what was sown!

A VISIT TO WALES

We'd heard about its beauty,
We'd read the stirring tales,
Seen pictures of its mountains,
And so we went to Wales.

We saw the lakes at Rhyader,
Admired the lovely scenes,
We climbed the top of Snowdon,
Looked down into ravines.

We visited the castles.
Picnicked beside a rill,
Enjoyed the lovely valleys
Until we'd had our fill.

We then returned to Sussex,
Where we belong by birth,
We halted at South Harting,
Stepped out on Downland turf.

We saw the gentle landscape,
Looked out toward the sea;
My wife sighed with contentment,
"Good old Sussex" murmured she.

THE SWALLOW'S MESSAGE

High up in the heavens a dark speck I see;
Can that have, I wonder, a message for me?
Yes, twisting and turning, fast scouring the sky,
The first of the swallows is searching for fly.

We welcome the bird with the tiny black wings
Because of the message of joy that it brings,
For gone is the winter with all its sad train,
The swallows are here, and it's springtime again.

Yes, summer is near, with its train of delights,
Its long sunny days, and its warm scented nights,
The skylark is singing its song of good cheer,
The children are shouting, "The swallows are here".

Ah, give me the summer, with rabbits at play,
When squirrels make merry the whole of the day,
The songthrush and blackbird sing forth their delight,
And nightingales trill in the dead of the night.

The sights, scents, and sounds of the summer, I find,
Are like a clean tonic to freshen the mind,
With fragrance of roses to perfume the way,
And scent in the meadows of newly mown hay.

So welcome, sweet swallow, though short is your stay,
We know in our hearts you are British alway,
The birds of the tropics you look on with scorn,
For all of our swallows have been British born.

And when in the autumn away you must fly,
To live in the warmth of South Africa's sky,
We'll think of you kindly through all winter's pain,
And live for the day when we see you again.

THE SILENT PRESENCE

A little child may be beside
   His mother all the day,
Yet seldom speak a word, because
   He's busy with his play.

He knows that while his Mum is near
   There is no cause to fret,
Her presence far removes all fear;
   His needs will all be met.

His mother may be busy too,
   And she may seldom talk;
She has too many things to do
   To take him for a walk.

She also knows that he is there,
   Quite safe within her sight,
So both are happy, and can share
   In mutual delight.

Just so, the child of God may know
   His Father's presence here,
While busy with the things below
   He feels that Heaven's near.

He may not have the time to pray
   Upon the bended knee,
But silently, throughout the day,
   He upwards sends a plea.

And so in all life's common things,
   Each different path that's trod,
The presence of the Saviour brings
   Sweet fellowship with God.

BEING RETIRED

Rejoice, O young man in your strength,
The freshness of youth's morning dew,
The days have not sufficient length
For all the things you have in view;
For youthful zest, by vision fired,
Knows not the bane of being tired.

But as the days slip quickly by,
The years seem short, the hours seem long;
From time to time one heaves a sigh,
Where once was naught but merry song,
For as one's mortal powers decay
Then tiredness comes at close of day.

But when one passes sixty five,
Though interests still range far and wide,
We're thankful then to be alive,
For many youthful friends have died;
Then one feels tired at morning light –
And oft RE-TIRED before 'tis night.

Then, if on earth we've come to know
The God of Hope and Calvary's cross,
Who can eternal life bestow,
For which we count this world but dross,
Then, when life's gone, we'll reach that shore
Where tiredness will be known no more.

THE CHAPEL MOUSE.
or
The Preacher's Lament

If you through Heathfield make your way
    towards the Sussex Downs,
Turn off through sleepy Rushlake Green
    far from the busy towns.

You'll wend your way through country lanes,
    by cottage small and neat,
Until, in sight of Windmill Hill,
    you come to Bodle Street.

The chapel there is plain to see,
    with schoolroom in the rear,
Where God's good word has oft been preached
    to all that come to hear.

'Twas there I went one autumn day
    to preach the word of life,
But what began in peace and joy
    became a scene of strife.

For as I preached there came a stir;
    some folks began to smile:
And I my bold contender saw -
    a mouse came up the aisle!

Church mice, they say, are poor and weak,
    for they have naught to eat;
But Chapel mice are flourishing,
    and quick upon their feet.

For Sunday dinners, chapel teas,
    bring tit-bits sweet and rare,
Which Mr. Fieldmouse loves to add
    to his more dainty fare.

This mouse was such a doughty foe,
    his eye was bright and keen;
He ran across a lady's toe -
    and quite transformed the scene!

He boldly marched up to the front;
    he stood up on his toes,
Then looked at me defiantly
    and wrinkled up his nose.

Close to him, by the organ seat,
    were two young ladies fair,
But they were being quite discreet -
    they never turned a hair.

The three boys sitting in the back
    were all agog to view,
And even father could not quite
    suppress a smile or two.

I tried to get attention back
    to focus on the text
But one thought seemed in every mind -
    "Where will he pop up next?"

Although I to my subject warmed -
    the fire within me burned;
As I was teaching others, I
    myself a lesson learned -

That if the preacher wants to gain
    attention from the house,
He'll find he's on the losing side
    competing with a mouse.

The OIL-CAN

I tell you the tale of a funny old man
Who always took with him a little oil-can,
When he went out walking he often would stop
Inspecting gate hinges, and give them a drop.

When he was invited to come in a home
He'd peep round each corner like some little gnome,
He'd be most delighted to find a jammed door,
Then out came his oil-can to give it a pour.

When once through the door he'd inspect the inside,
To see if the bolts there would easily slide,
And how he would chuckle if one was too tight,
For out came his oil-can to make it just right.

The boys with their go-carts thought he was a joke,
Inspecting the wheels, whether solid or spoke,
If one started squealing as though it was hurt,
He'd take out his oil-can and give it a squirt.

They called him eccentric, and so that may be,
But he has a lesson to pass on to me,
To take my own oil-can of kindness and cheer,
That when I find troubles - my oil-can is near.

A COUNTRY PREACHER

Among the many stories
  that old Sussex folk can tell
Are those of country preachers
  who had served their chapels well.
They walked for miles on Sundays
  to their chapels far and near,
Where rich and poor would gladly
  come these humble men to hear.

One such a man was Tandy,
  of the real old country type,
But Tandy had a weakness,
  for he loved his 'bacca pipe'.
One day he was accosted
  with his pipe beneath his nose,
Sniffing the fragrant spiral
  from his 'bit of twist' that rose.

"Got yer old idol going,
  Master Tandy, there I see",
One of the Pub-crowd ribbed him,
  while the others laughed with glee.
"I fear it is an idol";
  and the old man shook his head,
"But then, I bid ye notice,
  I be burning him," he said.

Mark well, and learn the lesson!
  It's convenient if not nice,
When yielding to a weakness
  to make virtue out of vice:

LIGHTS THAT SHINE

The Fiery Sun

God made the fiery burning sun
By his almighty power,
A silent witness to his might
It shines on hour by hour.

If God's creation shines so bright
We scarce can bear to gaze,
What beauty, purity, and light,
In God himself must blaze?

And what holds up that mighty world
Which light and heat doth give,
Three hundred thousand times as great
As this on which we live?

It is the hand of Him who formed
And set it on its way,
We see the sun, by what it is
Still praises him each day.

It praises him by what it does
In giving heat and light,
Without the sun, our earth would be
In one perpetual night;

For every blade of grass that grows,
Each tree, each opening flower,
Can only grow because it feels
The sun's life-giving power.

Lights that Shine

The Stars

If this our sun should praise the Lord,
What of the distant star?
Each is a sun, as large as ours,
And some are larger far.

They in their countless thousands shine,
A tribute to His might,
God set them also on their way,
And guides them through the night.

In countless numbers, there they spread,
Through endless realms of space,
He filled them with the energy
They need to run their race.

We ought to trust a God so great,
So faithful, and so wise,
He listens to an infant's prayer,
Although he built the skies.

The stars the vast expanse of heaven
In wild confusion fill,
Yet they their proper order keep
Because they do his will.

And so the stars should teach us trust,
They teach obedience too,
What anxious cares we would be saved
If we God's will would do.

Lights that Shine

The Moon.

The silent moon that rides the sky,
That beauteous queen of night,
Which sheds on earth its mellow rays;
Whence doth it draw its light?

It is a light which from the sun
Is handed down to us,
Which gives the moon its beauty rare,
And lights our darkness thus.

The moon her silvery beauty owes
To giving, full and free,
This simple lesson needs be learnt
By all humanity.

Just as she always does her best
To emulate the sun,
And do at night what through the day
His shining beams have done,

So we should always do our best
To follow Christ the Lord,
And help each other, cheer and bless,
In thought, and deed, and word.

The moon should oft remind us too
Of God's unfailing plan,
For every month it's waxed and waned
Since first the world began.

And so the Lord is never slack,
(Though we may sometimes fret),
He's never hasty, never late,
And never will forget.

Lights that Shine

The Glow-worm.

The same almighty hand that made
The sun in fiery strength,
That stretched the vast expanse of heaven,
In depth, and breadth, and length;

The hand that formed a million stars,
Beyond conception bright,
And set the moon above the earth
To rule the sky by night,

Has made the little glow-worm, with
Its tiny lantern bright,
Which fills the heart of young and old
With innocent delight,

He set it in the ditches, where
The sun, for all its might,
The stars for all their glory, and
Their penetrating light,

Or moon, with her more gentle rays,
Can never hope to shine,
It lights the hedgerow bottoms
Where the roots of ivy twine.

Yet though it's such a humble thing,
It serves a useful sphere,
And says to ev'ry passer by,
"My Maker put me here".

Lights that shine

Mankind.

Teach me these lessons well, O Lord,
And though my light is small,
Keep me from slipping backward, till
My light shines not at all.

May I in some small way reflect
The light that shines in Thee,
The mirror of my heart keep clean,
Though none are near to see.

For not until I am content
To be a glow-worm here,
Can I expect to be a star
In any higher sphere.

If as a glow-worm, or a star,
My light shines clear and bright,
May I remember, day by day,
Mine is a borrowed light.

For no man to himself can live,
Not all I have is mine;
For God, and man, each day will give
New light, to help us shine.

CRAFTSMEN OF THE BIBLE

The craftsmen of the Bible, how varied was their trade,
We love to read about them, and all the things they made
God gives all men their wisdom, some put it to good use,
Others from sinful motives, those precious gifts abuse.
As did the silver workers, who plied a busy trade,
While simple people worshipped the idols they had made.
But other silver workers and those who worked in gold
Made for God's tabernacle, things glorious to behold.
While those who used the needle made all the curtains fair;
The veil so richly broidered, and High Priest's garments rare.
It tells us of the baker, a butler who made good,
The blacksmith with his anvil, and those who worked with wood.
The busy potter, sitting beside his turning wheel,
By making pots and vases, displayed his art and skill.
We read about the sailors who sailed the ocean blue;
Of magistrates, and jailers, of many soldiers too.
The patient, humble fisher, who sets his simple sail
To catch the lightest breezes, or ride the roughest gale.
But most we read of Jesus, a servant he was made,
As carpenter he laboured, commending honest trade,
Though to His earthly parents He was both kind and true,
It was His Heavenly Father's great work He came to do.
That work He has accomplished, though at an awful loss;
He could not say "It's finished", till dying on the cross:
Now every needy sinner who on His work relies
Will see God's greatest Worker exalted in the skies.

FARMERS AND GARDENERS

The Bible tells of farmers, who by their patient toil,
Spend many hours in winning a harvest from the soil.
It tells us of their labours, the carter with his team,
The sturdy, patient ploughmen, with plough of wooden beam.

The smoother of the furrows, the sower of the seed,
Of men that worked with mattocks, and hedge-makers we read
It also tells of mowers who swung the scythe at dawn,
The wheat and barley growers, and reapers of the corn.

Of various forms of threshing, the winnowers of wheat,
The poor but honest gleaners who gathered ears to eat.
We read about the herdsmen, with cows and bulls of course,
Swineherds and camel drovers; the masters of the horse.

Of goatherds in the desert, and those who donkeys keep.
The ever-watchful shepherd, and shearers of the sheep.
Then there were vineyard keepers, the gatherers of fruit,
Pruners, and humble gardeners who fertilized the root.

The waterers and planters, and those who grafted trees,
The grape and olive pressers (the oil and wine from these),
Of those who gathered honey, and those who dug the wells
Of bird-scarers and hunters, of fowlers too it tells.

This worthy art of farming, the scriptures still declare,
Stems back to Adam learning in Eden's garden fair,
In this we see all people in Adam have a part,
For nearly all his offspring, are gardeners at heart.

THE PLOUGHMAN

Elisha, with twelve yoke of oxen,
Slowly turned the fallow ground,
By his strength and wisdom guiding
As the plough he followed round.

Early ploughs were rough and simple,
Trunks of tree, with iron shod,
Slowly pulled by labouring oxen,
Merely breaking up the clod.

Thus has man, throughout all ages,
Down from Adam's day till now,
Tilled the ground for various uses,
Winning bread by sweat of brow.

By his various inventions
Man the work has simplified;
Tractors, ploughs and rotovators
To the work are now applied.

Yet, for all man's skill and patience,
God alone can increase give,
And the proudest of earth's monarchs
On this humble toil must live.

Maybe on these thoughts, Elisha
Mused as round the field he trod,
For, we read, that close beside him
Walked unseen the man of God.

He had time for such reflection
As he slowly made his way,
Time for prayer, and meditation -
How we need it in our day.

The SOWER

A sower, bearing precious grain,
    Went out, so Jesus said,
To sow the seed, that he might gain
    A harvest, to make bread.
The sower on the path must throw
    Some seed, exposed it lay,
Then quickly came the cunning crow,
    And stole that seed away.

Some seed on stony ground then fell,
    Where earth was thin and light;
This germinated very well,
    The blades looked green and bright.
And yet, e'er many days were done
    They died, and bore no fruit,
But scorched and withered in the sun,
    Because they had no root.

And some seed fell among the thorn;
    But when the thorns grew high,
They choked the young and tender corn,
    And caused the ears to die.

But other fell on better soil,
    Deep-rooted, free from weeds,
The subject of the sower's toil,
    Preparing for his seeds;
The root went down and found good store,
    The blade grew strong and bold,
Some thirtyfold, some sixty bore,
    And some an hundredfold.

So may our lives reflect God's love,
    And in good works abound,
That at the last we each may prove
    We are not barren ground.

SHEPHERDS

For fear lest beasts their flocks should spoil,
The eastern shepherds kept
A constant watch, and wary toil,
While sheep in safety slept.

They little cared how rough the way,
What deep ravines they crossed,
But searched the mountains night and day
If one poor sheep was lost.

This David knew, and so he prayed
God would his Shepherd be,
To bring him back whene'er he strayed,
And guard him constantly.

He knew that shepherds had to seek
Fresh pastures every day,
Be ready to support the weak,
And show the flock the way.

He knew too, how they loved their sheep,
And called each one by name,
When he had Jesse's flock to keep
He doubtless did the same.

Much from his sheep could David learn
While working on the farm,
And trusted that his God in turn
Would keep him from all harm.

BUILDERS and BRICKMAKERS.

The Bible tells of builders
  who worked with brick and stone;
They made the greatest buildings
  the world has ever known.

Of how, beside the river,
  they made their bricks of clay,
Mixed in the straw and stubble,
  and baked them day by day.

Some worked as slaves for Pharaoh,
  the pyramids they built;
Some raised the 'hanging gardens'
  beside Euphrates' silt.

Some built the mighty temple,
  and humble homes as well,
The rich and ornate palace,
  where kings and princes dwell.

They cut down mighty cedars
  for rafters in the roof,
Then covered them with plaster
  to make all waterproof.

We read about a city
  whose builder is divine,
Where all who trust in Jesus
  will see His glory shine.

STONEMASONS

We read of those who built of stone
The greatest buildings man has known,
From pyramids, and stores for grains,
To humble homes, roadways, and drains.
Much skill they need this work to do,
For varied are the stones they hew,
Some large, some small, some flat, some squared,
Each one for its own place prepared.

Some into lovely shapes are carved,
And some prepared to be engraved,
Some for the step, the corner too,
Foundation stones, quite hid from view.
The types to work are strange enough,
Some hard, some brittle, soft and tough,
Some light, some dark, some red, some tan,
Find use beneath the tools of man.

We see the work they did so well,
And think of God who gave them skill,
For all true wisdom God imparts,
Though often to unthankful hearts.
When Solomon the temple reared
Stones great and costly were prepared,
The masons in the quarry hew,
And silently the temple grew.

Our God Himself a Mason stands,
Exceeding skilful are his hands;
He takes men from their ruined state
A living temple to create.
Though we of hearts like marble fret,
All stained with sin, and black as jet,
God can these stony hearts remove
And give us His new heart of love.

THE CARPENTER OF NAZARETH

We read of many carpenters
And much work that was done,
But, other than the Saviour,
We've name of only one.
This just, but humble worker
A noble task was given,
To be the earthly father
Of God's dear Son from heaven.

It may be many tradesmen
Achieved more fame than he,
But none could be more prayerful,
Or show more piety.
His life was interrupted
By constant change and flight,
Moving as was directed
By God in dreams at night.

His tools were very simple,
He took them as he moved,
And by his daily labours
Supported those he loved.
We read about the hammer,
The marking line, and rule,
Of planes, and saws, and compass
The file, the axe, the awl.

No doubt the youthful Jesus
Would use those tools as well;
We think of Joseph working
Beside Emmanuel.
O may we be like Joseph,
Whilst working, often pray,
And feel the Saviour's presence
Beside us every day.

SHIPBUILDERS, SAILORS, and CARGOES

All they that go down in their ships to the sea.
   That trade in deep waters and great.
The wonderful works of the Lord they can see,
   And wonderful things can relate.

We read in the Bible of how ships were made,
   The shipboards of fir trees bespoke,
The masts, made of cedar, by tackling were stayed,
   And oars made from toughest of oak.
Fine linen from Egypt was brought for the sail,
   Embroidered with purple and blue,
An anchor was made to be used in the gale,
   A rudder to guide the ship true.

We read of the men who engaged in the trade.
   Of caulkers who made water-tight.
The sailors who managed the vessel when made,
   And pilots to guide them aright.
King Solomon's navy sailed over the blue
   While seeking for rich merchandise,
They brought gold from Ophir, and ivory too,
   With cinnamon, oil, balm and spice.

They brought him fine horses, with peacocks and apes.
   All manner of raiment and wool,
Strange packets from merchants, all sizes and shapes,
   With precious and costly gifts full.
Fine emeralds, coral and agate they bring,
   Their treasures both costly and rare,
With all kinds of metal, from silver to tin,
   And food from the countries afar.

Though vast was the treasure that came in each load,
   Far greater than words can denote,
The greatest of treasures which God has bestowed
   Was found in a fisherman's boat.

The TEACHER

By the lake our blessed Master
 taught the people by his word;
As they pressed upon him faster,
 He could not be clearly heard.

Two small ships, as used for fishing,
 Jesus saw there, close at hand;
One of these he entered, wishing
 to be thrust forth from the land.

Many people now came thronging
 to the Galilean shore,
For their hearts were full of longing,
 wanting him to teach them more.

Lovely stories he was teaching,
 of the simple things they knew,
He, through these, their hearts was reaching
 with a message, deep and true.

Would you now their joy inherit?
 Then you need not travel far,
For he still speaks through his Spirit,
 and can teach you where you are.

FISHERMEN

Beside the sea of Galilee
The Saviour saw the fishnets spread,
Where the two sons of Zebedee
Worked to produce their daily bread.

The hardest work that men engage
Must surely be the fishers' toil,
They have to face the tempest's rage,
While angry waters round them boil.

With skill to guide their ship aright,
Patience and courage they display;
Perhaps to toil all through the night,
Yet still have nought at break of day.

Many the fishers by that lake,
Who sailed their boats upon the sea,
But unto four the Saviour spake,
Bid them, "Leave all, and follow Me."

Peter and Andrew, James and John,
Were those that heard his voice, and fled
From boats and nets, and so became
Fishers of human souls instead.

Jesus these humble fishers sent:
His servants still today are taught
How they can cast the gospel net,
That many may to God be brought.

May sinners yet be gathered in
From this polluted, carnal world,
Saved from the deadly power of sin
To that new life in Christ our Lord.
Then let us for God's fishers pray,
That souls be gathered now, as then,
And others hear the Saviour say,
"Come, follow Me, and fish for men."

The MASTER FISHERMAN.

Seven men I see are fishing
 on the wild Tiberian wave,
Toiling, rowing, casting, wishing,
 not a single fish they have.

Soon the morning sun is waking,
 filling earth and sky with light;
Ruefully, they stock are taking,
 not a single fish in sight!

Hark, a stranger now is hailing,
 "Children, have you any meat?"
Sad, they tell him of their failing,
 they have nothing fit to eat.

But he bids them yet be cheerful,
 "Cast your net again" he cried,
Cast it forth, and don't be fearful,
 cast it out on your right side".

Changed is now their sad behaviour,
 as in hope their net they throw;
They remember how the Saviour
 bade them cast three years ago.

Will they witness a repeating
 of that first, most wondrous pull?
Yes! Their hearts are strangely beating
 as they see the net is full.

He who drew the fish, where falling
 net could gather such a haul,
Now the souls of men is calling -
 greatest Fisherman of all.

THE HOME GUARD

"We'll fight them on the beaches,
We will fight them in the fields,
We'll fight from woods and ditches,
We will never, never yield!"

Our hearts were stirred within us
As brave Churchill spoke for all,
And so the Home Guard mustered
As the leaves began to fall.

We carried our own shot guns,
Some could two-two rifles bring;
While some had nought but courage,
Yet they rose to serve the king.

"If the Germans do invade us
Then a motor-bike will come,"
They said to me, "And fetch you";
For we had no phone at home.

It must have been turned midnight;
I was wakened by a noise:
'Twas someone on a motorbike!
I listened for a voice.

My heart was palpitating,
When I heard the self-same roar
- It was my brother Billy
Letting out a mighty snore!

THE LITTLE CORPORAL

We had a little corporal,
Billy John-Bull was his name,
Who, though was nearly eighty,
Thought he still was just the same
As when he joined the army,
While a youth, to see the world,
And went to every country
Where the Union Jack unfurled.

I loved to hear the stories
That old Billy could relate;
How he was sergeant major,
When he stood at five foot eight.
He'd fought the Sikhs in India,
Went through the First World War;
But now, at nearly eighty,
He had shrunk to five foot four.

One day we were assembled
With the tallest on the right,
Preparing a manoeuvre
That would leave an even sight,
With the tallest on the outside,
And the centre sloping down,
To cut a better figure
As we marched through Crowborough town.

As I stood to attention
With old Billy by my side,
He viewed the situation
With a bit of British pride:
He said, "What a fine body
In the infantry we make;
For I am next to smallest
- And I am five foot eight!"

ATTENTION!

We were to be inspected
By a Brigadier one day
Our unit was assembled,
And we made a fine array.

We had polished up our buttons,
Shone our boots as though inspired,
Our forage caps were angled
In the way the book required.

Said the Colonel in his pep talk,
"Put the Coldstreams in the shade,
And show the coming Brass Hat
We're the HOME GUARD on parade!"

Old Billy was promoted
To control that day's parade;
With his sergeant major's training
He for this was tailor-made.

He <u>was</u> the sergeant major:
Every inch of five foot four,
His grizzled lips were parted
For a sergeant major roar.

He went to shout **"ATTENTION"**
That would bring us to our toes
- And caught his flying dentures
Some two feet beyond his nose!

FOR SUCH A TIME AS THIS

We read that when God's people
  were in such deep distress,
He raised them up Queen Esther,
  "For such a time as this."

And so in nineteen-forty,
  when Britain stood alone,
He raised up godly leaders
  who would His honour own.

King George inspired the people,
  when all was black as night,
That trusting God Almighty
  was better than a light.

God gave him heavenly wisdom
  to call for days of prayer,
When all that those around him
  could see, was black despair.

Such was the time of Dunkirk;
  God made the sea a calm,
So tiny boats could carry
  our soldiers safe from harm.

While Air Chief Marshal Dowding,
  who led Fighter Command,
Spoke of God's intervention,
  and of His guiding hand.

And famous Douglas Bader,
  of courage and cool head,
Also God's hand acknowledged,
  and this is what he said:

"The fifteenth of September,
  the Battle in the air
Was won: it was a Sunday."
  - It followed days of prayer.

The mighty German Army,
  with tanks and guns galore,
On land was yet unbeaten,
  all set to win the war.

But God called able generals
  who feared Him, to the fight,
Monty and Alexander
  in Africa unite.

In General Slim of Burma,
  a man of prayer we see,
And noble Alexander,
  Lord of the Admiralty.

The vital Isle of Malta
  was held against all odds,
"But," said good General Dobbie,
  "The victory was God's."

So turned the tide of battle,
  while thousands fought and died,
And many, in the turmoil,
  on God alone relied.

And so God demonstrated
  the truth which makes secure:
"Sufficient is Thine arm alone,
  and our defence is sure."

A TRIBUTE TO KING GEORGE VI.

Written on the day of his death.

It was not by the will of man,
But in accordance with God's plan,
 That George our King became;
The wisdom of it now is seen,
For with his good and gracious Queen,
No English monarch more has been
 Revered than he in name.

His hand was placed upon the helm
When darkest clouds o'erhung our realm,
 And yet he did not flinch:
Against the evil he withstood,
A staunch supporter of the good,
And when the foe came like a flood,
 He never gave an inch.

When black as night the war-clouds grew,
He did the faintest heart renew,
 By noble act and word;
He bade us trust the God of love,
Which better than a light would prove,
And did the fear of night remove
 From all of us who heard.

For fifteen years the crown he wore,
For fifteen years the burden bore,
 Though fraught with toil and strain;
And though by weakness oft assailed,
His post, with all that it entailed,
He nobly filled, not once he failed,
 Throughout his noble reign.

Although he bore a weakly frame,
He was a king in more than name,
  He fully played his part;
Though some the kingship may despise,
This king was good in all men's eyes,
He had what men most highly prize,
  A great and noble heart.

A pattern for us all he stood,
In doing what a Christian should,
  The whole of his life through;
His throne maintained in truth and right,
He boldly trod the darkest night,
He kept the faith, he fought the fight,
  As kings should always do.

"Upon that man" our God has said,
"That honours me, I'll surely shed
  A lasting, rich increase;"
And our late king was ably shod,
To fear not man, but only God,
Thus, when the path of death he trod
  He proved his end was peace.

He was a man who walked with death,
And yet feared not its icy breath,
  Nor faltered at the end;
His life hung on a slender thread,
But Death, that foe which some men dread,
Came to him as he slept in bed,
  And proved to be a friend.

A just man now has passed away,
Whose memory shall not decay,
  But always linger on;
On English life his hand did trace
A mark that time shall not deface,
And in our hearts he has a place,
  Though he himself is gone.

With solemn pageant him they bring,
A funeral as befits a king,
  And yet we know withal,
Whatever monument they raise,
Or epitaph to sound his praise,
The shrine that most his worth displays,
  Is in the heart of all.

A noble loyalty, well proved,
To God, to man, the land he loved,
  In him was always seen;
May we who mourn this solemn day,
In which our king has passed away,
That selfsame loyalty display,
  To our young, gracious Queen.

THE BUGLE

A ploughboy heard the bugle,
His horse on the bit piece champed;
It sounded out from Buckhurst
Where the army was encamped.

    Hark, I hear a bugle calling,
Clearly rising, softly falling:
Borne upon the evening breezes,
Who can tell what heart it teases?
Notes that speak to some, contentment,
Fill another with resentment:
Whilst those notes, so freely ranging,
In their tempo ever changing,
Mingle with the dews of evening,
Who can fail to tell their meaning?
Laughing notes, and full of folly,
Sober notes, and melancholy;
Brazen notes, the world defying,
Notes that speak of brave men dying;
They can fill the heart with gladness,
Or can make it melt with sadness,
For it is the bugle's glory
It can tell a moving story.
    Now its notes are loudly ringing!
In my mind I see men springing,
Springing up in answer to it –
Men in former days who knew it;
Knew it in the early morning
As the light of day was dawning,
Knew it in the midst of battle
Sounding o'er the musket's rattle,
Knew its notes and message clearly,
Knew it well, and loved it dearly.

The Bugle

Old soldiers hear it ringing;
Its sound they had come to know,
Floundering in the trenches
Where the Flanders poppies grow.

    See the ploughman weary treading,
With his horses homeward heading,
Hears the notes he's ne'er forgotten,
Head and back instinctive straighten,
Whilst his footsteps change and quicken
As by inspiration stricken;
Quick his horses sense his waking,
Toss their heads, their bridles shaking
Arch their necks, and show their graces
As he puts them through their paces
While its notes, alive, untiring,
Man and beast alike inspiring;
Thus the bugle stirs and hustles,
Gives new life to tiring muscles.

What of the little schoolboy,
With his cap and coat awry,
Wandering slowly homeward
As the day goes flying by?

    Schoolboys listen to its measure,
Hear the notes with unfeigned pleasure,
Hearken spellbound to its trilling,
Think a soldier's life is thrilling;
Laugh to hear its mad careering
And are brightened by their hearing.
For those notes, so bright and cheerful,
Banish every thought that's fearful;
Not for them the scenes so gory,
All they think about is glory;
E'en the timid ones grow bolder,
Each resolves to be a soldier.

The Bugle

Sight-seeing in the Army!
Africa, India, Rome;
Far from the lonely vigil
Of the woman left at home.

    See the widow, in her cottage,
As she makes her humble pottage
Hears the notes of sorrow telling,
In her eye a tear is welling,
As she hears the notes that sounded
O'er the fallen and the wounded:
So her mind goes back afore-time
To the dreaded days of wartime,
When her husband, for his nation,
Fought and died in some far station:
In a humble grave they laid him,
There a rugged cross they made him,
But a cross that's harder, rougher,
Is the one his wife must suffer.

On the parade ground wheeling
Soldiers all acting as one,
Trained to repress all feeling:
- Each one is some mother's son.

    Here a mother, busy cooking,
Through her kitchen-window looking,
Sees her husband in the garden
Where the work his hands must harden;
Clear as lark they hear it ringing,
Yet another message bringing,
Halts them in their work and pleasure
As they think of their lost treasure:
Like twin pigeons, homeward winging,
In two minds one thought is springing,
Why do nations tear each other,
Killing husband, son, and brother?
Nations rise! and stop this madness,
Filling homes with so much sadness.

The Bugle

Pause now, and ask the question,
Will it always speak of strife?
Is war the only answer
To the problems of man's life?

    Peaceful efforts all will crumble
Till man's heart is made more humble,
Naught from threat of war will ease us
But to have the mind of Jesus,
When his kingdom is extended,
Then shall greed and hate be ended.
Christ shall come, the once rejected,
Purging earth by sin infected,
And the things which now so tire us,
Warfare, weed seeds, germs and virus,
All effects of sin and Satan
Shall be banished 'neath his baton;
All his foes shall be refuted,
And the busy bugle muted;
But the final trumpet sounding
Tells of a new era's founding,
And His word, who holds the seven
Stars, shall make new earth and heaven:
Heaven and earth beyond our telling,
Righteousness alone there dwelling.

THE LIFE OF DAVID

The angry lion on him turned,
And o'er the stripling shepherd reared;
David all thoughts of safety spurned,
But caught him by his tawny beard.

And so he killed the dreadful foe,
Likewise, a bear that came to rob
Was killed by David, with a blow
From his strong arm, and shepherd's rod.

THE LIFE OF DAVID

1. Who David was.

David of whom the Bible tells
Was Jesse's youngest son;
Of eight fine sons this good man had,
He was the fairest one.

When David was a shepherd lad
And kept his father's sheep,
He led them through the sandy plains,
Or on the mountain steep.

He grew from childhood into youth,
Much grace did God impart;
'Twas said of him he was a man
Formed after God's own heart.

David became a mighty king,
A fearless soldier too,
And in the Bible we may read
Of things he used to do.

A poet with a tuneful voice
Was David all his days;
The Psalmist sweet of Israel,
Who loved to sing God's praise.

2. The LION AND THE BEAR.

An eastern shepherd, with his sheep,
Would wander far, by night and day;
A watchful eye would always keep,
Because of birds and beasts of prey.

Through rugged country they would roam,
Where'er the mountain grasses grew;
Through deserts wild, which were the home
Of prowling bears, and lions too.

And so it was, as David went
With Jesse's flock, to find their keep,
A lion came, with fierce intent,
To make a meal of David's sheep.

When David saw, he did not pause,
But ran, before it was too late;
He forced apart the lion's jaws,
And saved one from a cruel fate.

The angry lion on him turned,
And o'er the stripling shepherd reared;
David all thoughts of safety spurned,
But caught him by his tawny beard.

And so he killed the dreadful foe,
Likewise, a bear that came to rob
Was killed by David, with a blow
From his strong arm, and shepherd's rod.

I have no doubt but that he prayed
To God for strength, and courage too,
For he declared t'was by God's aid
That he the bear and lion slew.

3. DAVID the DELIVERER.

Who is this that curseth Israel?
Who is this defies the Lord,
Boasting in his brazen armour
His own strength, and his own sword?

'Tis the mighty son of Anak,
Nine feet tall he proudly stands,
Like a weaver's beam the spear-shaft
Which he carries in his hand.

"Who will fight with proud Goliath?"
Daily is the challenge sent:
Israel's heart is turned to water;
Saul is hiding in his tent.

Lo! The stripling son of Jesse,
Stout of heart, though slight of limb,
Bringing cheeses to his brothers,
Sees the situation grim.

David said, "Why are ye fearful?
Why is all the host dismayed?
He who fights Jehovah's battles
Will receive Jehovah's aid.

What! Shall he defy Jehovah!
God, who mighty things has done:
He who drowned the hosts of Pharaoh,
Shall He be subdued by one?

Shall he curse the God of Israel,
He the Lord of Hosts defy,
And escape the dreadful vengeance
Of our God, the Lord Most High?"

Thus he reasoned with the people,
And to Saul they quickly run:
"We have found the Lord's deliverer,
David, Jesse's youngest son".

Saul as quickly sent for David,
God's deliverer to thank,
When he saw the youthful shepherd
Then his heart within him sank.

"Lo" he said, "Thou art not able
Victory o'er this man to get,
He has long in war been skilful,
Thou art but a stripling yet".

Then, so quietly, David told him
Of himself he made no boasts,
But his faith was wholly founded
In his God, the Lord of Hosts.

"See" he said, "My God delivered
To my hand the beasts of prey;
Will he not likewise the heathen
Who has cursed His name this day?"

Then the king brought forth his armour,
Placed his sword in David's hand:
David thought them little value,
Though the finest in the land.

"No" he said, "I cannot use them,
Though no doubt they're very good,
For myself I've never proved them
As I've proved my faithful God."

Thus, divested of Saul's armour,
Boldly forth the stripling trod,
Armed with just his staff and stone-sling,
And a simple faith in God.

None, in fact, had better armour
Than had Jesse's son that day!
Clothed in God's divine protection,
Little did he fear the fray.

From the brook he chose his pebbles,
Put them in his shepherd's purse;
Though Goliath railed upon him,
David heeded not his curse.

"You have come with spear and buckler,
With your sword upon your side;
But my strength's entirely founded
On the God you have defied.

All assembled here shall witness,
It is not by spear and sword
That the Lord will save His people,
But by trusting in His word."

Thus spake David, and, unerring,
Swiftly did the pebble go,
Smote the boasting giant's temple,
Deeply sank, and laid him low.

Vain the breastplate and the helmet,
Vain the shield and greaves of brass!
Sword and spear will never alter
What the Lord will bring to pass.

Think, my friend, upon this stripling,
And the faith he had in God;
Trust the Lord to fight your battles
As you tread the heavenly road.

Trust not in another's armour;
Use no other's sword or spear:
Faith alone must be your buckler,
Arm yourself with constant prayer.

Trust in Him whom David trusted,
Ask His help to watch and pray,
And he surely will deliver
From the giants in the way.

4. DAVID'S ANOINTING.

Samuel was much dejected
When he heard the Lord declare,
"Saul as king I have rejected;
Now to Bethlehem repair.

Take the horn of holy ointment,
One of Jesse's sons I choose,
I alone make this appointment,
Hurry! There's no time to lose".

Samuel went to call on Jesse,
And God's word to him declared;
All but David were invited
To the feast they had prepared.

Seven sons, all handsome creatures,
Seemed to fit a kingly part;
God said, "Look not on their features,
I, the Lord, but read the heart."

First to come was tall Eliab,
He was Jesse's eldest son,
The next was called Abinadab;
Neither chose the Lord this one

One by one they disappoint him,
Then the shepherd boy we see:
"This is he! Arise, anoint him;
This my chosen king shall be."

Samuel poured the holy ointment
Over David's head of hair,
And, confirming God's appointment,
He received God's Spirit there.

5. DAVID FLEES FROM SAUL.

David fought in many battles
For his king and master, Saul,
Wise, though youthful, brave yet courteous,
Soon he was beloved of all.
Saul, they said, has slain his thousands,
David has ten thousands slain;
Maidens, dancing with their cymbals,
Sang aloud the sweet refrain.

Saul began to eye his servant,
Jealous thoughts soon filled his heart;
Till he, in a fit of anger,
Tried to kill him with a dart.
But the God whom David trusted
Guarded him by day and night,
And the people well approved him,
Wise in counsel, brave in fight.

David wed the king's own daughter,
And his son-in-law became,
But he found Saul's jealous anger
Was toward him just the same.
When at last it was reported,
"David lies there, sick in bed."
Saul in exultation ordered,
"Bring him here, I'll strike him dead,"

When the soldiers came to find him,
Through the window David fled,
While his faithful wife, to fool them,
Placed an image in the bed.
David had to leave his master,
He a fugitive became,
But he found, through each disaster,
That his God was still the same.

6. DAVID MADE KING.

What the news from Mount Gilboa,
Where the battle raged so long?
David told the sad, sad story,
In a soul lamenting song:
All the host of Israel fled,
Saul and Jonathan lay dead.

Then the leading men of Judah
Came to David in their need,
Saying, "We remember Samuel
Said you would be king indeed."
So, while choirs of Levites sing,
David is anointed king.

Yet the northern tribes of Israel
Still refused to hear God's call,
But, upon the death of Abner,
David came to rule them all;
Thus did God his word fulfil
Placed his king on Zion's hill.

God has yet a greater purpose,
Seen by type in David's life,
For His chosen, Jew and Gentile,
Long have been engaged in strife,
But, in gospel days we see,
Both made one through Calvary

Though the heathen raged together,
As foretold, and as was done,
God has placed a greater kingdom
Under David's greater son,
And has set, despite man's ill,
Christ upon His Holy Hill.

7. DAVID'S KINDNESS.

Behold how pleasant 'tis to see
When brethren dwell in unity;
When love and kindness fill each breast,
And stand the strain of every test.

Thus David loved the son of Saul,
His Jonathan, so brave and tall;
Their mutual love did firm abide,
Though Saul to part them often tried.

When Jonathan in battle died
David in bitter sorrow cried;
"His love" he said, "So firm and free,
Was very wonderful to me."

The pact of love which David made
With Jonathan, was now displayed,
In that he for his children sought,
And for his sake, much kindness wrought.

From this a lesson we should take –
Do others good for Jesus' sake;
We cannot give to Him, that's plain,
But many of His house remain.

If Christ were here on earth once more
Would we not share with Him our store?
Would we not give, nor count the cost,
To Him who came to save the lost?

What now you owe to Jesus, give
To those with whom you work and live;
Your loving care their path can ease –
This is the way we Him can please.

8. "HE RESTORETH MY SOUL". Psalm 23 v3.

Thus David wrote, and 'twas a truth he proved,
For he had wandered from the God he loved;
Set his own heart on carnal things of life,
And sadly sinned against a man and wife.

Yet his great Shepherd did not leave him there;
But Nathan sent, a Prophet, and a Seer,
Sent him to bring His foolish, lost sheep back,
And set his feet once more upon the track.

The prophet told of how a wealthy man
Took from the poor his only precious lamb,
And dressed it for a visitor to eat,
Being too mean his own flock to deplete.

"That man shall die!" The king in wrath began,
But Nathan said, "O king, thou art the man!"
Thou art the man! The truth of what was said
Came to the king, in shame he bowed his head.

What bitter grief, what sorrow then was known:
Judged meet for death, in God's sight and his own,
And though the Lord pronounced his sin forgiven,
See how he poured his spirit out to heaven.

Read through the Psalm we call the fifty-first;
See how his heart with shame and sorrow burst!
He owned himself a sinner base and vile,
Unworthy of the heavenly Father's smile.

Do not our hearts with David here agree?
Is not our prayer "Be merciful to me."
Wash me, O God, and make me clean within,
Oh, purge me from the curse of indwelt sin.

He prayed the hyssop on his heart might lie,
That little shrub which must the blood apply;
So we the Saviour's precious blood would plead,
Apply it, Lord, to all who feel their need.

9. What David sang.

Psalm 23.

The Lord my tender shepherd is,
No wants have I, or needs;
He makes me lie in pastures green,
Beside the stream He leads.

He watches o'er my wandering soul,
And He restores the same;
He leads in paths of righteousness,
For sake of His own name.

Yea, though I walk the vale of death,
No evil will I fear,
Thy rod and staff, they comfort me,
For Thou art ever near.

Thou hast my table richly spread,
In presence of my foes;
With oil Thou dost anoint my head,
And my cup overflows.

Thy goodness, mercy, and Thy love,
Shall follow all my days,
And then, for ever in Thy house,
I'll dwell to sing Thy praise.

CHRISTMAS-TIME

Christmas is a welcome time,
  Of laughter and good will,
The sights and sounds of Christmas' past
  Refresh our memories still.

The wonder, beauty, peace and joy
  Of this most blessed night,
Captures the hearts of young and old
  With innocent delight.

But the real joy, the meaning true,
  Of our festivity,
Is in the Son of God Himself,
  And His nativity.

He only is the one who brings
  True joy and peace on earth,
Love to our hearts, for God's own love
  Is seen in Jesus' birth.

He is the reason voices sing
  "Joy to the world is shown";
"Glory to God in highest heaven"
  Our lips make gladly known.

So may the treasured Gift of God
  Be yours on Christmas day,
May happiness, with blessings rich,
  And love, be yours alway.

For He who was in stable born,
  Laid in that manger bare,
Will come and dwell in every heart
  Which longs to have Him there.

THE MAGNIFICAT

My soul now magnifies the Lord,
   My spirit still rejoices
In Him, my Saviour and my God,
   Who spoke by angel voices.

For He has had regard to me
   His servant-maid so lowly,
All generations me shall see
   As blessed by God most holy.

The Mighty God great things does here,
   For one of lowly station,
His mercy is on those who fear
   In every generation.

His arm of strength has now been shown
   Against the proud and flighty,
He scatters them, and from the throne
   He has put down the mighty.

The lowly ones He sets on high,
   The hungry fills with plenty,
Those who were rich in days gone by
   Are now returning empty.

He helps his servant Israel's clan,
   His mercy faileth never,
As spoken once to Abraham,
   And to his seed for ever.

HANNAH'S SON

Poor Hannah was sad, for she hadn't a son.
    While others had daughters as well,
She thought in her heart she would ask God for one,
    And all her unhappiness tell.

Her husband was kind, but he seemed not to know
    How deep was her sorrow and care,
She said, "To the temple of God I will go,
    And make it a matter of prayer.

As there she stood praying, not uttering a word,
    Old Eli the priest came along,
He saw her lips move, but no language was heard;
    He judged her - but there he was wrong.

For Hannah soon told him the grief of her heart,
    God gave him a message of joy;
Jehovah was taking this poor woman's part,
    And promised her long-hoped for boy.

So Samuel was born at the time God had said,
    But what would she do with him now?
She'd loved to have kept him at home, but instead,
    She gave him to God in a vow.

Then, Oh what a song from dear Hannah burst forth,
    When Eli the child had received;
Her full heart rejoiced with the purest of mirth,
    And blessed was she that believed.

A day to remember; A day to rejoice;
    A day to praise God for His word:
Not only to render her thanks with the voice,
    But yielding her all to the Lord.

The GOSPEL according to JOHN chapter 1

In the beginning was the WORD,
and the WORD was with God,
and the WORD was God.

All things were made by him;
and without him was not anything made
  that was made.
In him was life;
and the life was the light of men.
The light shone in the darkness,
and the darkness comprehended it not.
That was the true Light,
which lights every man that comes into the world.

He was in the world,
and the world was made by him,
but the world knew him not.
He came unto his own,
and his own received him not.

But as many as received him,
to them gave he privilege to become
  the sons of God,
even to them that believe on his name:
which were born, not of blood,
nor of the will of the flesh,
nor of the will of man,
but of God.

The WORD was made flesh,
and dwelt [tented] among us,
(and we beheld his glory,
the glory of the only begotten of the Father,)
full of grace and truth.
Of his fulness have all we received,
and grace for grace.
For the law was given by Moses,
but grace and truth came by Jesus Christ.

THE STRANGER AT THE DOOR

Among the desert dwellers
　came a stranger all alone;
He seemed so poor and humble,
　with no riches of his own,
The custom of the desert was
　that he should be received;
Made welcome in their goat-skin tents,
　and have his wants relieved.

But no one would receive him,
　he found every tent door closed,
Until one humble dweller felt
　his heart kindly disposed,
And welcomed in the stranger,
　though himself was very poor;
The man had showed such patience
　as he waited at the door.

Those in this tent were quite prepared
　to give him everything,
Then found, to their amazement,
　they had entertained the king!
Of all the people, small and great,
　they were the only ones
To whom he gave the privilege
　of being called his sons.

When they believed his promises,
　and trusted in his name,
He opened up his treasure chests
　and shared with them the same;
Instead of losing what they had,
　they gained abundant store;
And all because they welcomed in
　the stranger at the door.

THE GIVING OF THE LAW

See the lightnings o'er the mountain;
  hear the mighty thunder roll;
Smoke ascending like a fountain,
  striking terror to the soul.
Hear the voice as trumpet sounding,
  waxing louder, louder still;
Through the mountain range resounding
  God is speaking from His hill.

There before the mountain, quaking,
  Moses and the people stood,
While the holy God is making
  Known His will, for Israel's good.
With this mighty demonstration
  of His holiness and awe,
God instructs His chosen nation
  by the giving of the Law.

Moses quakes, yet is ascending
  up the smoking mountain wall,
Fear, and love, and worship blending
  as he nears the God of all.
Then, upon the stony tables
  God wrote down the ten commands,
So unlike the foolish fables
  used as laws by other lands.

Thus the moral law was given,
  what man must, and must not do,
All who keep this law from heaven
  find that blessing will ensue.
Though the scene described was fearful,
  though the words themselves are stern,
All who make their study careful
  will the love of God discern.

"Love worketh no ill to his neighbour: therefore love is the fulfilling of the law." Rom. 13 v10.

THE TEN COMMANDMENTS
(Abbreviated)

Listen to God's firm decree,
You shall have no God but Me.

I the Lord am God alone,
Make no idol out of stone.

Never lightly use God's name,
But revere and bless the same.

On the holy Sabbath day
You must put your work away.

Children parents must obey,
Honour them from day to day.

Let not anger rise until
There is felt the urge to kill.

Adultery is a dreadful sin,
With a look it can begin.

Though temptation's power you feel,
You must never, never, steal.

You shall not false witness bear,
Tell a lie, or curse and swear.

Covet not your neighbour's store,
Ever reaching after more.

The Law is more than a moral code. It is as much an integral part of social life as the laws of nature are essential to creation. Those who transgress this law will as surely suffer the consequences as those who disregard the law of gravity and step off the edge of a cliff. Only a miracle could save a falling body, and only a miracle of grace can save the fallen soul.

THE ELEVENTH COMMANDMENT

In the bonny land of Scotland, very many years ago,
Up to the parson's doorway came a stranger, old and slow;
His steps were very feeble and his hair was snowy white,
A'begging for his supper and a lodging for the night.

He soon was welcomed gladly, for the minister was kind,
The wife also was happy for she knew her husband's mind;
The old man soon was eating at the humble parson's board,
And after having supper there was reading of the Word.

It was the lady's custom every night to catechise,
She wanted all her household to be made salvation wise:
"How many the commandments?" Then she paused his face to scan;
"I think there are eleven" said the humble little man.

What righteous indignation did she shower upon him then;
"Shame on you Mr. Stranger, you should know there's only ten!"
The old man listened meekly, as the lady warning gave
Of being still unready, though so very near the grave.

Next morning very early e'er the parson's wife had stirred,
The sound of praise and praying in the garden shed was heard,

The minister came softly, and found there upon his knee,
The stranger of last evening, and heard his gracious plea.
The little man was pleading at his heavenly Father's throne,
All lost in adoration, and most reverent his tone,

"Pray who are you my brother" said the minister with awe,
"For no one nearer heaven in their prayers I ever saw."
"I've been ordained the bishop of this diocese", said he,
"And so have come in secret my parishioners to see."

The minister requested, on the coming Sabbath day,
That he would preach the sermon, and the bishop answered "Yea,
But let not your good lady know the secret that we share,
Nor how you have discovered that I lead a life of prayer."

So on the Sabbath morning, to the good dame's great surprise,
She found the humble stranger was the bishop in disguise.

The text that Sabbath morning was the Saviour's new command,
He called it the eleventh, and beneath God's gracious hand
He showed how that dear woman could the Saviour's words extol,
By feeding well his body, and by caring for his soul.

THE PEARL OF GREAT PRICE

We read about a merchant
Our Lord declared was wise,
He scorned all imitations,
And only good would prize;
Good pearls alone, he wanted,
So far and wide he sought;
This pattern we must follow,
Nor spend our strength for nought.

If we would seek things better,
Then we must search the field
Of God's own word, the Bible,
Rich treasure that can yield,
And treasure well worth finding -
Pearl of a heavenly prize,
It's said of all who find it,
"Made to salvation wise".

For Jesus is this jewel,
This pearl surpassing rare;
'Tis love, 'tis grace, 'tis purity,
That makes His face so fair;
Oh, precious, precious Saviour,
O may I call Him mine,
Would I could love Him better,
And to his will resign.

This pearl beyond all others:
Could I but prize Him more,
His beauties trace and cherish,
His wondrous love explore;
Could I but view him clearer,
Then, come whate'er betide,
I'd part with all life's treasure,
To have Him by my side.

EPHESIANS 3. 14-21.

I bow my knees to thee my God,
   my Father and my Friend,
In whom heaven's family is named,
   to earth's remotest end;

O grant that I might know within
   Thy Spirit's grace and power,
That Christ might dwell within my heart
   by faith, from hour to hour.

That being deeply rooted in,
   and grounded on thy love,
I might receive, and with thy saints,
   Thy choicest blessing prove.

The breadth, the length, the depth and height
   of Christ's own love to know,
Which passeth knowledge, yet is known
   by humble souls below.

That, being emptied of myself,
   and filled with love divine,
I shall Thy fulness, Lord, receive,
   and to Thy glory shine;

For thou canst do through us far more
   than we can ask or know,
That unto Christ be glory given
   by His own church below.

Isaiah 26 vv1-7

In that day shall this song be sung
   In all the land of Judah,
And ransomed souls of every tongue
   Shall raise Their hallelujah.

Our God a holy city built,
   Its walls are all salvation,
To guard from Satan, sin, and guilt,
   By Christ's propitiation.
Fling open wide the golden gates
   With shouts of exultation,
The city where Jehovah waits
   To greet his righteous nation.

That man a perfect peace has known
   Whose mind on God is grounded,
Because he trusts in God alone,
   He'll never be confounded.
Trust in the Lord when troubles rise,
   When clouds are overcasting,
For in the Lord Jehovah lies
   A strength that's everlasting.

The Lord will bring the haughty down,
   Lay low the lofty city;
The humble shall with honour crown,
   And on the poor take pity.
The Lord his people's path can weigh,
   He matches shade with brightness,
For he, most upright, is their stay,
   And leads them in uprightness.

And in that day it shall be said,
   This is our God and Saviour,
We've waited for our glorious Head,
   Now glad is our behaviour.

ISAIAH 28 v24 - 26

Does the ploughman plough all day,
Doing nought but turn the sod;
Turning this, and then that way,
Breaking up the barren clod?

No! He smooths the furrowed soil,
Makes the surface soft and plain,
Makes it fit, by loving toil,
To receive the precious grain.

Does he sow just rye and wheat?
No! He has a proper plan,
Growing various foods to eat,
For the benefit of man.

And shall God, who made man wise
To fulfil this ancient art,
Not some glorious way devise
Dealing with the sinner's heart?

Though He brings conviction's plough,
Breaking up the barren ground,
Making haughty weeds to bow,
Weeds of evil which abound,

Yet the Spirit's gentle rain,
And the gospel's soothing voice,
Heals the broken heart again,
Makes the barren to rejoice.

Many promises are sown,
Many precious fruits to eat,
But, whatever else is known,
Jesus is the Princely Wheat.

INCREASE OUR FAITH

Oh, give me faith, more living faith,
    The gift that God has given,
That draws its life from Jesus' death,
    And takes the soul to heaven;
Give me that faith of which a grain
    A mighty mountain moves;
Which makes the rugged places plain,
    The crooked spot removes.

I read the words where some expressed
    A humble faith divine,
And so to God made my request,
    That their faith might be mine;
I viewed the pathway which they trod,
    My heart within me failed;
The road that brought them near to God
    By grief was oft assailed.

I saw the crosses which they bore,
    Of persecutions great;
Of tribulations, sorrows sore,
    In body, mind and state;
'Twas thus they learned to love the Lord,
    And thus did faith increase,
By trusting only in his word
    They found surpassing peace.

And so I know not what to pray,
    (More faith I do desire,
Yet how my flesh dislikes the way,
    And shrinks before the fire).
May I be helped to watch and pray,
    Whate'er my portion be,
And humbly walk th'appointed way
    The Lord sees best for me.

GETHSEMANE

Lord fill my soul with strong desire
    to know more of your love,
Make my poor heart to heaven aspire,
    and set my thoughts above;
In sovereign love, Lord, you came down,
    a humble babe was born,
And thus exchanged your heavenly crown
    for earth's cruel crown of thorn;
O may my heart dwell more on this,
    to melt its native ice,
That Christ, to bring us home to bliss,
    made such great sacrifice.

Into the garden I would go
    where men the olives dress,
And there, by humble faith, would view
    Christ in the olive press;
Gethsemane! What does it show?
    - a Saviour bruised and pressed,
From whom rich streams of grace now flow,
    that sinners may be blessed;
The Saviour learned obedience there,
    though he was God's own son,
Lord, grant me grace to use his prayer,
    "Father, Thy will be done".

Men bound him with their cruel cords,
    and spit upon his face,
The King of Kings, and Lord of Lords,
    there took the sinner's place;
Lord, move my heart to weep with thee,
    and touch compunction's cord,
As, gazing on Gethsemane
    I view my suffering Lord:
But I may read, and hear, and learn,
    yet still remain the same,
Oh, make my spark of love to burn,
    and burst into a flame.

P recious are the promises,
   God's own word declares them so,
   Only those who feel their need
   Come their preciousness to know.

R egal are the promises,
   Given by the King of Grace,
   And he of his bounty gives
   Unto all who seek his face.

O urs may be the promises,
   If we plead in Jesus' name,
   God the Father has declared
   That he will fulfil the same.

M any are the promises,
   For they cover every need,
   So whatever is our case
   There is one which we can plead.

I nfallible the promises,
   Though the hosts of hell assail,
   For our God has sovereign power
   Which assures not one will fail.

S weet are all the promises,
   Fragrant with the Saviour's grace,
   All to seekers freely given,
   Though of Adam's fallen race.

E xhaustless are the promises,
   Springs that never will run dry,
   Every generation proves
   They contain a full supply.

S ealed are all the promises,
   By the Saviour's precious blood,
   Shed for us at Calvary,
   Reconciling us to God.

THE THORN

Lord, take away this thorn,
'Tis more than I can bear;
It makes me weak, and worn,
And fills my heart with fear:
But though God's servant wept and cried,
It festered still within his side.

O Lord, this thorn remove;
Once more he made his plea,
That I may useful prove
In winning souls for Thee;
But still no answer he received,
And still the pain was unrelieved.

Lord, take this thorn away!
I cannot still maintain
My work to watch and pray
While bearing so much pain;
It makes me weak beyond belief,
O quickly send me some relief.

And then the Lord replied,
I will not take away
The thorn from out your side,
I have a better way;
My grace sufficient for your aid,
My strength in weakness perfect made.

Ah Lord, 'tis now I see
In weakness I can boast,
Thy power will rest on me,
And I will owe Thee most;
Thus Paul would prove, nor he alone,
A thorn more blessed than a throne.

HONOURABLE SCARS

"I know," said Mr. Valiant, as he gained the land of
  light,
"My scars I carry with me as the trophies of my fight,
For I have fought His battles, Who once fought the
  fight for me,
And gained the scars of victory as He died upon the tree."

I too was sorely wounded, and that sore ran in the
  night,
I could not stop its fester, though I tried with all my
  might,
Each time I thought about it I could feel the inward
  pain,
And when I had forgotten, it would open up again.

But then I saw my Saviour, kneeling in Gethsemane,
"Not my own will, my Father, but that which pleases
  Thee".
For there He was forsaken, who had shown man nought
  but good;
Did others now forsake me? - there was reason why
  they should.

In Him there was no reason, yet He bore it patiently,
And I had heard His promise, of My grace I give to
  thee;
I bowed my head in sorrow, for I saw my pride was
  hurt,
Whereas my blessed Saviour with humility was girt.

Yes, I have scars in plenty, but I trust they all are
  healed
By Him who bore my sorrow, and to whom I had
  appealed.
Now I can look upon them, and am happy in the thought,
"My scars I carry with me, for His battles I have fought".

SORROWFUL yet always REJOICING

Miss Sorrow had great beauty, like leaf-bare winter trees,
Set out against the sunset as night begins to freeze,
Her voice was low in singing, though sweet as nightingale,
Her lip would often tremble, her face, though fair, was
 pale.
Joy too, possessed a beauty, but his was bright and fair,
With gladness in his laughter, and sunshine in his hair;
His voice soared up when singing, as lark upon the wing,
His face was that of victor, his bearing, that of king.

We never can be wedded, said Sorrow with a sigh,
My path lies in the valley, your's takes the road on high.
Yes, mine is in the sunlight, said Joy, 'Tis sad to tell,
We cannot be united, but part with fond farewell.
Then, over both, came stealing the presence of a King,
One who had borne much sorrow and yet of joy could sing;
A holy awe so filled them, that to His feet they came,
They bowed their heads in worship, and breathed
 Immanuel's name.

As King of Joy I see Him, said Sorrow through her tears,
A crown of glorious victory upon His head appears,
The scars He bears so clearly, that glorious victory prove,
I feel my sorrow melting before His wondrous love.
No, Sorrow! Joy said softly, The King of Sorrows He;
The crown that wreathes his forehead is made of thorns,
 I see,
For He has borne man's sorrows, by dying to atone,
And yet He brings such gladness the world has never
 known.

Then we are one in Jesus! We can united be,
For Joy and Sorrow mingle, in Christ, at Calvary:
They hand in hand went forward, blest in their Lord's
 employ,
For those who know deep sorrow, may yet be filled with
 joy.

The OLD PATHS

"O stand ye in the paths and see",
Ask for the pleasant paths of old,
The paths of Gospel liberty
Which God's Word only can unfold;
The paths the holy fathers trod,
The paths that bring the soul to God.

Ask for the path of Living Faith,
Born of the Spirit's quickening breeze
The life that's drawn from Jesus' death,
No other life our God can please;
The path that makes his precepts bright,
Whene'er we have to walk by night.

Repentance is the path to seek,
For all who seek, shall surely find
A peace of soul in spirit meek,
A holy joy in humble mind;
Ask then, for God to turn you round,
And make his holy fear abound.

Obedience to the law of God,
Submission to his holy will,
This also is a pleasant road,
Though often-times it leads uphill;
The Lord himself this pathway trod,
And sealed obedience with his blood.

These are the paths that lead to God,
Old paths they are, and yet how sweet,
They're beaten tracks, that formed the road
For countless saintly pilgrims' feet;
But if you have an interest there,
These paths are only trod by prayer.

Mark well these paths; yet you will prove
The best of all the paths is LOVE.

BROTHERLY LOVE

Of all the natural blessings that were given unto man
by God, the source of goodness from above,
In all his life there's nothing that can give more
pleasure than the power, and capacity to love.

But who can tell the wonders of this blessing so
divine, or who can even half its merits tell?
For if we take away the love, our lives, however
fine, are empty as a cast-up seashore shell.

'Tis little acts of kindness which can help us all
along, 'tis love that makes the daily burden light,
And though our hearts are heavy, we can often burst
in song, when thoughtful acts of love come into sight.

Yes, God is love, and when he made the first man
long ago, and in that form of dust inspired his breath,
He breathed in of his nature, of his love, for this we
know, that perfect love is stronger far than death.

If we but read our Bibles well, then we shall surely
find examples of this truth in God's own word,
Like Jonathan and David, who were men of loving
mind, whose hearts were knit together by the Lord.

Nothing is so touching as the love a mother shows
for her children, for the offspring of her womb.
And nothing makes the prodigal return, but that he
knows a love for him still permeates his home.

Yes, love is such a powerful thing, I wish that all the
world would practise love, and let her virtues free,
And over every summit, let her banner be unfurled,
For men, to walk together, must agree.

CHARITY

True Charity is so much more
Than human love, or kindly gift;
'Tis Love in Action, which to God
Can giver and recipient lift.

If I on human eloquence,
Or angel's tongue am borne along,
And have not this, I am become
As tinkling cymbal, sounding gong.

If I have gift of prophecy,
All knowledge of God's secret will,
A faith which mountains can remove,
And have not this, I'm nothing still.

Should I give all to feed the poor,
Or yield my life on fiery cross,
And have not this, the Love of God,
Then all I do is counted loss.

Love suffers long, is always kind,
True charity no envy bears,
Does not parade itself for show,
Is not puffed up with haughty airs.

Is never rude, nor seeks its own,
Is not provoked, nor evil thinks,
In what is wrong cannot rejoice;
Truth only with rejoicing links.

It bears all things, believes all things,
It hopes the best, whate'er prevails,
Though sorely tried, it still endures –
This is the Love that never fails.

"TRUST...IN THE LIVING GOD
Who giveth us all things richly to enjoy.

God has given everything
 freely for man to enjoy;
As the harvest fruits we bring,
 product of a year's employ
We rejoice in all He sent,
And in honest labour spent.

Freely shone the sun on high,
 likewise fell the gentle dew;
While an ample food supply
 from the soil all nature drew;
Freely every blessing flowed
On the labour man bestowed.

For the beauty of the flower,
 for the life within the root,
For the scent which fills each hour,
 for the various kinds of fruit,
We thank God, who helps man toil
To bring food forth from the soil.

Oh what joy the seed to sow;
 in the ground it must be cast,
Then what joy to see it grow,
 and the harvest reap at last;
God alone the seed can bless,
Yet man labours for success.

Freely God his loved Son gave,
 freely came the Son to die,
To redeem all from the grave
 who upon his grace rely,
And, as seed cast in the clod,
Now commit their souls to God.

THE LORD LOOKS AT THE HEART

You should not judge your fellow man
    by clothes that he is wearing;
A well-made suit can sometimes give
    a rogue a regal bearing:
An honest heart may often beat
    beneath a coat in tatters,
And always in the sight of God
    it's character that matters.

The company a person keeps
    may sometimes pick the winners,
But Jesus Christ was wrongly judged
    because He mixed with sinners:
And Jesus was the Son of God,
    of love the very essence,
And sinful lives He still transforms
    just by his very presence.

Nor can we ever best assess
    a man by his relations:
Cain killed his brother, yet came from
    the holiest of nations;
Don't judge a man because his speech
    is poor, or has a stutter,
For evil thoughts may hide behind
    a speech as smooth as butter.

Nor make the man who may have failed
    the subject of your censure;
Some are too honest to succeed
    in this world's business venture:
And many thought th'apostle Paul
    a failure, not success,
Yet he received the Lord's "Well done",
    and crown of righteousness.

WHO IS THIS?

He rode on the foal of a donkey,
"Hosannah", the multitude cried,
For blest is the King who is coming
Of whom it was thus prophesied.

"Hosannah" (Lord save us), they're shouting,
They sing in the height of their bliss,
But rulers and priests stand there doubting,
And wanting to know, "Who is this?"

This One is the man of God's choosing,
A Saviour to come to man's aid,
To suffer, through wounding and bruising,
When on Him our sins would be laid.

This One is the Son of the Father,
Sent down from the glory above,
Who came with the Father's commending,
The wonderful gift of His love.

This One is the King of all nations,
Who comes in the fulness of days,
To gather from all of life's stations
A people to form for His praise.

This One is the Priest God anointed
To stand in the poor sinner's place,
To offer Himself, as appointed,
That we might be saved by His grace.

This, then, is a most searching question,
Can I say, "This One is my King,
My Saviour, my Advocate, Master,
And to Him my homage I bring?"

LOADING THE VESSEL

There is no valid reason
  not to ask for greater things
When coming with petitions
  to our God, the King of Kings;

If we come with faith undoubting,
  courage God's own word to take,
Wait with patience for His answer
  as we ask for Jesus' sake;

Wisdom, guidance, strength and courage,
  full supply for all our need,
God has promised to believers
  when in Jesus' name they plead.

AND SETTING THE SAILS

Though we can't create the breezes,
  nor control the way they blow,
We can set our sails to catch them,
  and direct the way we go;

Though we can't command the Spirit,
  we may bow before the Lord,
Set the sails of our affections
  as He teaches in his word;

Then the storms that we encounter
  will but bear us on our way,
Guided by the Spirit's breathing
  we shall sail to endless day.

THE SONG OF MOSES

The Lord God of Israel has fought gloriously,
The horse and his rider he cast in the sea;
No God can compare with Jehovah, the Lord,
No enemy stand in the face of his word.

The women of Egypt shall sorrow and weep,
For all Pharaoh's captains are drowned in the deep,
And Pharaoh himself, with his chariots of war,
Has sunk like a stone by the deep Red Sea shore.

The hand of Jehovah is glorious in might,
His right hand subdued all the forces of night;
He dashed them to pieces who stood in the road,
That Egypt may know that the Lord, He is God.

All those that against him rose up to rebel,
He, by his own greatness, could easily quell,
His wrath, which went forth like an all-burning flame,
Consumed them like stubble who scoffed at his name.

His power issued forth as a terrible blast,
And into a heap all the waters were cast,
The depths were congealed by the might of his hand,
To make for his chosen a path of dry land.

The enemy said, "I will hotly pursue,
My hand shall possess them, their leaders subdue,
And when I have caught them, and taken the spoil,
This army of slaves shall return to their toil."

God blew with his tempest, and straightway again
The waters came rushing back over the plain.
These caught the Egyptians, who sank as though lead,
The deep Red Sea waters closed over their head.

Though others have gods, yet our God is the Lord,
He only true refuge and help can afford;
Most glorious in holiness, fearful in praise,
None else can compare with the Lord's mighty ways.

The mercy of God I will sing all the day,
Who brought forth his own in a wonderful way,
To guide them by strength to the land he declared
From ages eternal for them was prepared.

The people of Canaan shall sorrow for fear,
When they of the might of Jehovah shall hear;
All Edom shall tremble, their Dukes 'twill amaze,
When they hear the tale of the Lord's wondrous ways.

The strong men of Moab will tremble and shake
At thought of the arm that did Pharaoh o'ertake;
Yes, all of their people will wither away,
For God's mighty arm will prevail in that day.

The host of their armies in terror shall stand,
As still as a stone under God's mighty hand,
Till all of his people, redeemed by the blood,
Have finished their journey, and crossed Jordan's flood.

Yes, God will establish them by his own hand,
And cause them to dwell in his most holy land,
As trees will he plant them, to grow in his ways,
And cause them to bring forth rich fruit to his praise.

The Lord will then reign as their God and their King,
And praise in his house they will constantly sing,
They'll tell of the glory which he has displayed.
For with such a Saviour, who could be afraid?